C000145224

21st CENTURY LATIN

Sam Foster

summersdale

21ST CENTURY LATIN

Summersdale Publishers Ltd
46 West Street
Chichester
West Sussex
PO19 1RP
UK

www.summersdale.com

Printed and bound in Finland

ISBN: 1-84024-616-2
ISBN 13: 978-1-84024-616-2

21st CENTURY LATIN

From ASBO Teens to Being Green

Sam Foster

CONTENTS

Contenta

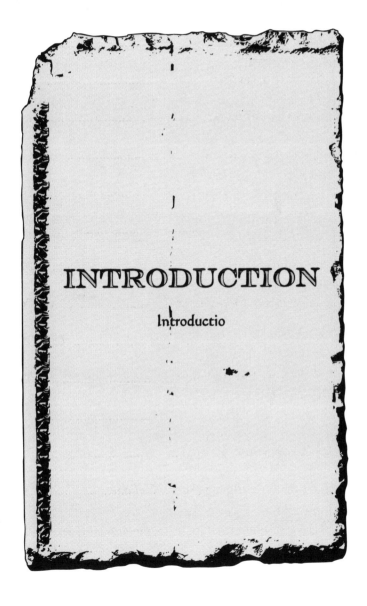

INTRODUCTION

Introductio

Hail, my fellow Latin-loving friends!

Most people's memories of learning Latin include grey-haired teachers and useful phrases like *Marcus est in latrina*, which they've never used since. But some of us have held on tight to this crumbling relic of a language in admiration, in the hope that one day we could breathe life into it again. Well, that day has arrived.

With Latin translations to suit every situation we modern folk find ourselves in, you'll never be lost for words. Whether you're complaining on holiday, buying a pint down the pub or just want to sound smart when you're at the office, then this book (and a few hours of practice) is just what you need.

So don your finest toga, wrap an olive branch around your head and step out into the twenty-first century, grasping your mobile-communication system (with high-speed Internet access, MP3 player and digital camera) and declare to the world: I speak Latin, you loser, and I'm proud!

And remember: Latin will only die if we do not speak it.

Salve, amici meii qui lingua Latina utuntur!

Homines qui linguam Latinam didicerunt recordant plerumque magistros capillis canis et locutiones utiles sicut Marcus est in latrina, quibus non utuntur ex hoc tempore. Sed nonulli nostri tenuerunt fortiter has reliquias friantes linguae admirantes et sperentes uno die posse inspirare vitam in eas rursus. Bene, hic dies advenit.

Cum translationibus aptis omnibus rerum statubus, numquam carebis verbis. Sive queror in feriis sive vis videri callidum esse in tabulario, hoc liber (et paucae horae exercitationis) sunt accurate quo cares.

Ergo, optimam togam indue, involve ramum olivae circum tempora et exi in saeculum vicesimum primum, tenens machinam communicationis in via (cum rapido aditu ad telam, lusore MP3 et camera photographica digitale) et declare mundo: Utor Latina, amittor, et superbus sum!

Et recordate: Latina solum cadet de usu si non ea utimur.

AT THE LOCAL

Tabernae Loci

If binge drinking was an Olympic sport,
Britain would get the gold medal.

Si bibere nimis esset ludus Olympicus,
tolleret Britannia clipeum aureum.

It's your round.

Vicis tua.

What's your poison?

Quod est venenum vestrum?

Two pints of lager and a packet of pork scratchings, my good man.

Duo sextarii lager et sarcinula scabationum porcinae, homo meus.

Anyone for a liquid lunch?

Aliquis est qui prandium liquidum vult?

Fancy a bit of karaoke?

Visne aliquid de carminibus in vice?

Cheers!

Salve!

There's not a pub quiz in town I can't win.

Non est aenigma tabernae in oppido quo non possum victoriam adipisci.

I'll tell you what makes a good pool player. Beer.

Dicam tibi quod te faciat bonum lusorem ludi globularum coloratorum. Cervisa.

This beer belly is living proof of a lifetime of philosophical contemplation.

Venter elongatus cervisa signum est vitae consumptae contemplatione philosophica.

Are you still serving food?

Adhucne victum ministras?

Three packets of Quavers please,
I haven't eaten.

Sarcinulae tres Quavorum
si vis, nihil edi.

I don't waste money on the
fruit machines. I sometimes win.

Non perdo pecuniam machinis frugis.
Nonnumquam vinco.

Stop touching my wife!

Desine tangere mulierem meam!

I think we should get married here.

*Credo nos debere matrimonio
coniungi hic.*

Put it on my tab.

Affer illud ad meam expensam.

CRIME
AND
PUNISHMENT

Crimen et Poenae

I never inhaled.

Numquam spirando duxi.

I guess murder is a crime; it depends which way you look at it.

Opinor caedem crimen esse; pendet de modo aspiciendi.

I was only holding my wife's champagne, your honour.

Tantum tenebam vinum spumantem camporum galliorum mulieris meae, honor tuus.

When you have a nice car, sometimes
you have to drive really fast.

*Quando bonum autocinetum habes,
aliquando debes id agere celerrime.*

Speed cameras ought to be illegal.

*Machinae photographiae celeritatis
debent illegales esse.*

Does it look like it fell off the
back of a lorry?

*Videtur similem esse aliquo quod
cecidit de autocarro?*

Community service is great fun; you feel
like you're giving something back.

*Ministerium commune bonus jocus
est; sentis se reddere aliquid.*

I can't talk right now; I'm just
driving past a police car.

*Non possum loqui nunc; vehor praeter
autocinetum vigilum.*

We find the defendant guilty
of crimes of fashion.

*Condemnamus reum de
criminibus modi.*

I'm writing a petition to Number Ten.

Scribo petitionem ad Numerum Decem.

I think my cat has been a
victim of identity theft.

*Puto felem meum victimam esse furti
qualitatis de qua cognosci potest.*

YOOF CULTURE

Cultus Iuvenum

Can I borrow your trainers?
These ones don't go with my tag.

*Possumne mutuuos sumere
calceos exercitii tuos?
Non apti sunt signo meo.*

Fight for the right to wear a
hoodie in supermarkets.

*Bellum agete pro liberatate
gerere tunicum cucullatum in
macellis communibus.*

If you can't get ahead, get an ASBO.

Si non potes progredi, ASBO capi.

We're going to drink some cider and spit
at people.

*Ibimus ad vinum ex malis confectum
bibendum et consputare homines.*

At least pay me to *stop* playing the guitar.

*Pecuniam da mihi saltem desinere
ludere cithira hispanica.*

And the point of scrubbing off
all the graffiti is…?

Finis detergendi titulos est… ?

Three McDonalds in the same high street doesn't mean a lack of choice. There's also a Burger King and a Wimpy.

Tres McDonalds in eadem via cardinale non facit egestatem delectus, est autem Burger King et Wimpy.

It's not litter, it's art – you have to learn to open your mind.

Non rejecta sunt, ars est – debes discere animum aperire.

I'm not stealing this car; I'm just doing my mechanics homework.

Non furor hunc autocinetum; facio opera facienda domi machinarum mea.

GARDENING AND HOME IMPROVEMENTS

Cura Hortensis et Correctiones Domus

Quick! Fetch me my trowel!

Rapide! Fer mihi asciam meam!

How can I join the local
allotment co-operative?

*Quomodo possum adiungi opere
commune locorum assignendorum?*

Be careful near the water feature.
It's a bit temperamental.

*Curam age prope fontem.
Aliquantum iracunda est.*

There's nothing quite like growing
your own vegetables.

Nihil est simile colendo holera sua.

We don't approve of poisoning the slugs.

*Non probamus venenum
dare cocleis pigris.*

It's not overgrown, it's rustic.

Non obsitus est, sed rusticus.

What hosepipe ban?

Quae prohibitio tuborum aquae?

It's not magnolia, it's vanilla mist.

Non est color magnoli,
est caligo vanilla.

How hard can it be?

Quam durum potest esse?

I like power tools – they make
me feel like a man.

*Mihi placent instrumenta potestativa
– me impellunt me sentire hominem.*

If a job's worth doing, it's worth doing well.

Si opus est dignus faciendo,
dignus est faciendo bene.

We had to get a man in.

Necesse erat nobis hominem inferre.

Why can you never leave IKEA with
what you went in there for?

Cur numquam potes ex IKEA
excedere cum eo quod
petens intravistis?

DINING
WITH
FRIENDS

Cena apud Amicos

I should've told you on the phone,
we're vegan.

*Debui tibi referre in telephonio, non
aliquid ex animalibus edimus.*

It must be sort of fun living in
such a small apartment.

*Debet esse ludi aliquid vivere
in tam parva insula.*

This is a colourful neighbourhood.

Est vicinia variata.

⟲

I put Viagra in the soufflés.

Pono Viagra aphrodisiaca in flatis.

⟲

Are you flirting with my husband?

Oscularis cum marito meo?

Not all of us can be Nigella Lawson.

*Non omnis potest esse
Nigella Lawson.*

Would anyone like to try the new hot tub?

Aliquisne vult tentare novum balneum calidum?

Shall we get take-out?

Abducamus cibum abducendum?

DINING OUT

Cena Foras

I'd like my eggs easy over, my bacon crispy, grilled mushrooms without the onions and brown whole wheat bread lightly toasted. Oh, and organic orange juice with pulp... and make it snappy!

Mihi placent ova faciliter versa, lardum fragile, fungi tosti et panis factus cum tritico integro leviter tostus. Oh, et sucus citrorum aurantiorum cum pulpa... et fac id rapide!

We're on a no-carbs diet.

Sequimur diaetam sine saccharis.

XL

I'd like my steak still bleeding.

Carunculae mihi placent adhuc sanguinem dantes.

My compliments to the microwave.

Gratias ago furno microundis.

I would send it back, but I'm scared you're going to spit in my food.

Remittam, sed timeo ne spuas in cibum meum.

Waiter, there's a fly in my soup.

Puer, est musca in iure meo.

I'm Ken, a chemistry graduate from Oxford, and I'll be your server this evening.

Ego sum Ken, laureatus chimica de Oxonia, ego ero minister tuus hoc vespere.

I'll just have a small fries.

Tantum exportabo parvam portionem solanorum tuberosorum frictorum.

Do you have any Peruvian ground almond
oil for my salad?

*Habesne oleum amygdalarum
Peruvianorum tritorum acetaria mea?*

I'm not usually one to complain but...

Non plerumque queror sed...

Cheque, please!

Perscriptio, si vis!

I can't remember my PIN. It's got nothing to do with that last bottle of wine.

Non possum recordari numerum propium quo cognoscar meum. Nihil attingit illam ultimam ampulam vini.

LEISURE

Otium

I want to be buried with my iPod.

Volo sepultus esse cum iPod meo.

I spend most of my weekends drinking virtual coffee with my friends on Second Life.

Consumo maximam partem vesperum meorum bibendo cafaeum cum amicis meis Secundae Vitae.

The remote control is like a comfort blanket.

Teleimperator est simile lodice consolanti.

I watch TV on Saturday afternoons to warm up for the evening programmes.

Tueor televisifica post meridiem diebus Saturni ut me exerceam pro prolaturis telvisificis vesperis.

I'm a dab hand at sudoku.

Aptus sum ad sudoku ludendum.

Is *Harry Potter* a suitable choice
for a book group?

Est Harrius Potter *delectus aptus
pro circulo librorum?*

Have you got tickets for Glastonbury?

Habesne tesseras pro Glastonbury?

Yes, it's a holiday, but it's also
an educational experience.

*Certe feriae sunt, sed etiam
experientia educens.*

Don't you think camping is
just so romantic?

*Nonne putas cubere in tabernaculis
valde amorificum esse?*

Did anyone bring the map?

Aliquisne portavit tabulam?

Is everyone having fun?

Omnis joco fruitur?

Why did you have to invite your parents?

Cur debuistis invitare parentes tuos?

EXCUSES, EXCUSES

Excusationes, Excusationes

I WOULD'VE COME BUT...
Venissem sed...

... I didn't want to leave the gerbil.

... non volui relinquere gerbillum.

... *Countdown* was on.

... Countdown *erat in televisifico.*

... I had to clean out the fridge.

... debui expurgare armarium frigidarium meum.

... I was in bed with two hot guys.

... eram in lecto cum duobus hominibus suavibus.

... there was a closing down sale at the pound shop.

... erat hasta claudendi tabernae assis.

... I couldn't find any underwear.

... non potui invenire subligar.

LIII

I CAN'T DANCE BECAUSE...
Non possum saltare quod...

... I have a wooden leg.

... habeo crus ligneum.

... people would feel uncomfortable.

... homines essent incommodati.

... there's not a pole.

... non est contus saltationis.

... I'm still sober.

... adhuc sobrius sum.

... I'm not wearing my tap shoes.

... non gero calceos leviter feriendi meos.

... I'd make you look bad.

... videretur malus.

I CAN'T GO OUT WITH YOU TONIGHT BECAUSE...

Non possum exire tecum
hac nocte quod...

... I'm washing my feet.

... *lavo pedes meos.*

... it would be against the law –
I'm a lot younger than I look.

... *esset contra legem – sum*
multo iunior quam videor.

... you look like my dad.

... *videris similis patri meo.*

... I can't find a babysitter for the quads.

... non possum invenire custodem puerorum pro pueris quadruplis.

... I might turn into a werewolf.

... fortasse fierer lycanthropus.

... my husband wouldn't like it.

... non placeret marito meo.

I CAN'T STOP AND TALK...
*Non possum sistere et
loquere ecum...*

... I'm in the middle of a
street theatre performance.

*... quod sum in medio de
una fabula in via.*

... I'm being followed by Russian spies.

*... speculatores Muscovitie
me consequuntur.*

... I'm late for my colonic.

... serus sum pro colonic meo.

... my wife thinks I'm having
an affair with you.

*... mulier mea putat me
adulterare tecum.*

... I'm late for my ASBO curfew.

*... serus sum pro fine vespertino
ASBO meae.*

... I'm participating in an
orienteering competition.

*... particeps sum certaminis
navigationis in cursu.*

I'M REALLY SORRY BUT...
Me valde paenitet sed...

... I sold your wife on eBay.

... vendidi mulierem tuam in eBay.

... I accidentally shot your cat.

... forte glandem emisi in felem tuam.

... I sat on your wedding cake.

... sedi in placenta nuptiarum tuarum.

... I didn't realise this was a funeral.

... non intellexi hoc esse funus.

... I ate all the chocolates.

... edi omnia dulcia de cocao.

... I played *Twister* instead of doing my homework.

... lusi Torquens in loco faciendi opera facienda domi mea.

... I got drunk and went to your brother's house... naked.

... bibi ad inebriationem et ivi ad domum fratris tui... nuda.

... I thought you said it was OK to have a party whilst you were away.

... credidi te dixisse id acceptabilem esse convivium habere quando foras esses.

... it'll never happen again.

... numquam accidet rursus.

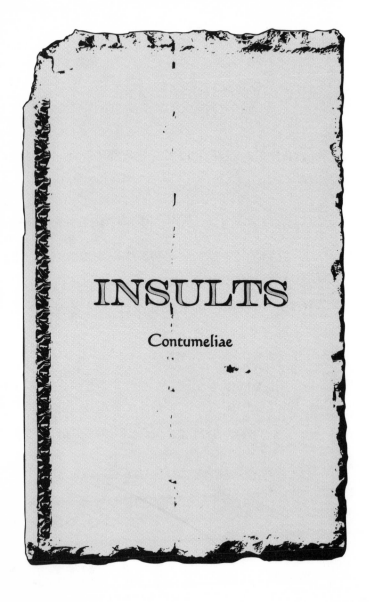

INSULTS

Contumeliae

Are you dribbling or do
you have a disease?

Salivas ut morbum habes?

You have the brain of a cheese sandwich.

Habes cerebrum sandwichi casei.

If you were twice as clever,
you'd still be stupid.

*Si esses bis tantum calidus,
stupidus esses.*

You pointless moron.

Moros sine proposito es.

Whatever, minger!

Quidquid, deformis!

I may be drunk, but in the morning I'll be sober and you'll still be ugly.

Fortasse ebrius sum, sed cras mane sobrius ero et adhuc deformis eris.

Please hide your face before I vomit.

Occulta faciem tuam prius quam vomam.

I'm talking to you, pal.

Loquor tecum, amice.

FAMOUS INSULTS

I fart in your general direction.
(*Monty Python and the Holy Grail*)

Mitto flatum ventris in regionem propinquam tuam.

What a tiresome affected sod.
(Noël Coward on Oscar Wilde)

Quis simulatus molestus cinaedus.

Unreconstructed wankers.
(Tony Blair on the Scottish media)

Masturbatores non-reaedificati.

Her face could launch
a thousand dredgers.
(Jack de Manio on Glenda Jackson)

*Vultus eius posset deducere mille
naves purgendi maris.*

You'd laugh at a Shakespearean comedy.
(Blackadder in *Blackadder II*)

*Inrideres comoediam
Shakespeareanum.*

FLIRTING ONLINE

Osculari in Linea

Do you visit this website often?

Frequentasne hoc situm telae?

Will you be my friend on Facebook?

Erisne amicus meus in Libro vultuum?

I still live with my mother.

Adhuc vivo cum matre mea.

How much money would I have to
pay you to kiss me?

Quantam pecuniam vis osculari me?

Do you like computers? I have a
really big hard drive.

*Placentne tibi computrata? Habeo
veram magnam memoriam duram.*

It's never going to work out – she's just
never been with a Mac user before.

*Numquam secundum erit – illa non
antequam fuit cum alicui
qui utitur Macintosh.*

I enjoy watching TV and eating too!

Mihi placet observare televisifica et edere simul!

I may be married but there's no harm in looking.

Quamquam habeo mulierem non nocet tueri.

My husband doesn't mind me flirting... with other women.

Non inritat maritum meum si osculor... cum aliis feminiis.

FLIRTING FUN

Otium Osculandi

You kiss like a washing machine on 'spin'.

*Oscularis simili modo machina
lavationis in orbem agenti.*

You're hot. I'm hot. I think it's pretty clear
what's going to happen here.

*Candens es. Candens sum. Puto
valde clarum esse quod accessurum sit.*

You may not think much of me now, but a
few more drinks and you'll be begging me
to take you home.

*Forte non aestimas me magni nunc,
sed paucae potiones plures et preceris
me te reducere domum.*

They say you have to kiss a lot of frogs
to find your prince. I've definitely been
around the pond a few times.

*Dicunt te debere osculari multas
anas invenire regulum tuum.
Certe circumivi lacum.*

Let's do some shots!

Faciamus nonullos iactus!

When I'm drunk I dance like a stripper.

*Quando ebrius sum,
salto modo denudatricis.*

I'm on the guest list.

Sum in indice hospitium.

Text me!

Manda textum mihi!

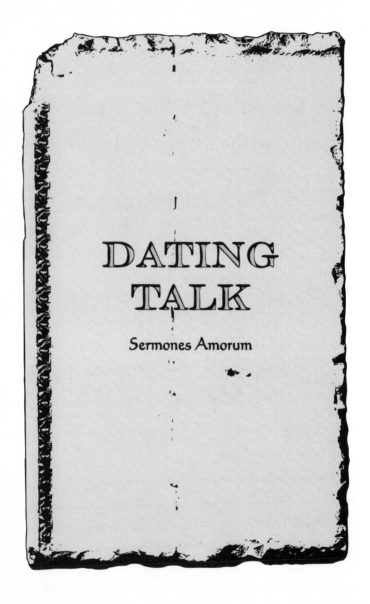

DATING TALK

Sermones Amorum

Can we skip the small talk
and just have sex?

*Possumusne transilire facetias et
solum coitum habere?*

Do you want to have
dessert back at mine?

*Vis adipisci mensas
secundias casae meae?*

You've got something in your teeth.

Quidquid habes inter dentes.

Speed dating is like all your worst
dates ever in one night.

*Agere assignationes rapidos
est consimile habendo omnes
assignationes pessimas suae
vitae una nocte.*

Sex with strangers is fine; it's sex with
people you know that causes problems.

*Coitus cum alienis innoxius est;
est coitus cum amiciis qui
facit difficultates.*

I never wear underwear on a date.

*Numquam porto
subligar assignatione.*

Why can't a rich old man and a beautiful
young woman be in love?

*Quis dicit id impossibilem esse senem
divitem et feminam pulchram
iuvenem esse inamoratos?*

My wives all get on really well.

*Omnes uxores meae vivunt
in concordia.*

Here's a photo of Michael when he was
two months old, and here he is
again at the park...

*Haec est photographia Michalis
quando habebat duos menses et
hic est rursus in horto publico...*

If I ask you to marry me, will you say yes?

Si te ores esse mulierem meam,
dicas vero?

I really like you.

Mihi valde places.

I wrote you a poem.

Scripsi poematem tibi.

So what are your views on
sadomasochism?

Quid putas de sado-masochismo?

THE TROUBLE WITH LOVE

Dolores Amoris

She mentioned the word 'babies'.

Dixit verbum 'infantes'.

She said she'd call me, but she
didn't ask for my number.

*Dixit se vocaturam esse me sed non
quaesivit numerum meum.*

He cheated on me so I posted a video
of him naked on You Tube.

*Coivit aliena femina, ergo posui eum
nudum in Tubo Tuo.*

We were going to get married but he didn't want to watch the *Big Brother* 24-hour live feed.

Nuptura eram ei sed ille non volebat observare Fratrem Magnum *totum diem et noctem.*

She wasn't replying to my e-mails, so I dumped her on MySpace.

Illa non respondebat mandatis telae meis, ergo abieci illam in MeaSpatione.

If I had to choose between my girlfriend
and my iPod, I'd choose my iPod.

*Si deberem optare utrum amicam
meam an iPod meum,
optarem iPod meum.*

He proposed to me in the
tinned food aisle at ASDA.

*Oravit me nubere sibi in area ciborum
in ollis stanni apud ASDA.*

Most marriages end in divorce,
so I'm not very optimistic.

*Matrimonia plerumque finiuntur cum
divortio, ergo non spero nimis.*

She got the kids, the house and the dog,
but I got the Porsche.

*Illa traxit domum, pueros et canem,
sed ego Porsche.*

It was an amicable break-up; the
restraining order saw to that.

*Erat divortium amicabile; prohibitio
congrediendi effecit id.*

We've broken up six times but this
time it's over for good.

*Reliqui illam sexies sed nunc
bene finitum est.*

MEETING THE PARENTS

Apud Parentes

I can see where Amy gets her good looks.

Video unde Amy trahit pulchritudinem.

What are my intentions?

Quo animum intendo?

I'm not sure about marriage; it's just a bit of fun at the moment.

Non certus sum de matrimonio; est ludi aliquid nunc.

I don't do any *hard* drugs.

Non utor duris pharmaceuticis.

May I call you `dad`?

Possumne te 'patrem' vocare?

If we have to sleep in separate rooms
then can we at least go and have
sex in that field now?

*Si debemus cubere in cubiculis
differentibus, possumusne exire et
coire hoc in agro nunc?*

That's not my mother, it's my sister.

Non est mater mea, est soror mea.

I know I seem like a real bore,
but wait till you get me drunk.

Have you got any pictures of
him as a baby?

Habes depictiones eius infantis?

I know I seem like a real bore,
but wait till you get me drunk.

*Cognosco me videri vere odiosum
esse, sed mane dum me videbis ebrium.*

I was thinking of breaking up with her, but now I've met you, I'm sure I will.

Putabam de relinquendo illam, sed nunc ubi cognovi vos, certus sum.

AT FAMILY
GET-TOGETHERS

In Conventibus Familiae

It's because we all live so far apart that I
appreciate my family more.

*Amo familiam meam magis quod
vivimus tam longe alii aliis.*

Do you think it's because we're inbred
that we all get on so well?

*Putasne nos tantos amicos esse
quod sumus incesti?*

I only go to family reunions so I can
see how fat everyone is.

*Tantum eo ad congregationes familiae
ut videam tam obesos omnes sunt.*

It's nice of your husband to come even
though you're cheating on him.

*Maritus tuus est benignus venire
quamquam adulteras.*

Steer clear of grandma, she always
tries to kiss you on the lips.

*Vitas aviam, semper tentat
osculari te in labiis.*

I think I was adopted.

Credo me adoptatum esse.

Well, it can't be worse than last Christmas.

Non potest peius esse quam proxima Saturnalia.

I've never liked turkey much, have you?

Numquam meleagridinas caras habui, et tu?

Don't forget to put your teeth in for dinner, mum.

Ne oblitus sis imponere dentes pro prandio, mater.

We used to all meet up for Christmas, but
now we just video-phone.

*Solebamus congredi pro Saturnalibus,
sed nunc tantum utimur televisiphonio.*

Dad, can you get the fire extinguisher? The
Christmas lights have blown up again.

*Pater, potes affere extinctorem ignis?
Lumina pro Saturnalibus
exploserunt rursus.*

I'm not sitting next to grandpa,
he has a flatulence problem.

*Non sedebo prope avum quod habet
morbum flatibus ventris.*

A wooden tie! It's just what I always wanted!

Ligneus nodus! Est cuius semper desiderium habui!

But we had turkey last year...

Sed habebamus meleagridinam anno proximo…

She's not got her hearing aid in.

Non habet auxilium audiendi in aure.

I've slaved over a hot stove all day
and none of you have even
touched your sprouts.

*Sudavi super focum calidum totum
diem et nemo etiam tetigit
brassicas oleraceas tuas.*

BIRTHDAYS AND WEDDINGS

Dies Natales et Nuptiae

50 is the new 40.

Quinquagies est novum quadragies.

The cocktail sticks are for eating the
sausages, not giving the dog acupuncture.

*Bacula sunt pro tumaculis edendis non
dare puncta cum acubus cane.*

Keep the drinks coming.

Persiste proferens potiones.

There were so many candles on the cake
they had to call the fire brigade.

Tam multi candelae erant ut
debuerint vocare vigiles.

Always the bridesmaid, never the bride…

Semper puella nuptae,
numquam nupta…

She looks like a meringue.

Videretur simile ovis percussis
et coctis in furno.

Weddings are the best places to meet
needy single women.

*Nuptiae sunt optima loca congredi
cum feminis solis carentibus amore.*

This is probably the wrong time
to tell you I'm gay.

*Non est tempus bonum tibi
dicere me cinaedum esse.*

We were worried he was
going to be deported.

Solliciti eramus ne deportaretur.

Civil partnerships are so much classier.

Nuptiae civicae sunt valde urbaniores.

ABROAD

Apud Gentes Externas

Spain would be so much better
without the Spanish.

*Hispania valde melior
esset sine Hispanicis.*

You have to go red first to
get nice and brown.

*Debes erubere primum
fieri vere fuscus.*

It was a last-minute deal on the Internet.

*Erat negotium de ultimo momento
temporis in tela.*

The hotel's a building site.

Hospitium est situs aedificandi.

I'll complain to *Watchdog* and demand my money back.

Conquerar Cane vigile et postulabo ut reddeant pecuniam meam.

There's a cockroach in my bed.

Est blatta in lecto meo.

Fucking mosquitoes.

Culicidae stuprantes.

This flight cost me £20 and there isn't even a complimentary packet of peanuts!

Volatus constetit viginti denariorum et non est etiam sarcinula libra arachidum hypogaearum!

(Said very loudly and very slowly)
Do you speak English?

Loquerisne linguam Anglicam?

I'm in Spain and my luggage is in Nepal.

*Sum in Hispania et impedimenta
mea est in Nepal.*

Cruises aren't just for old people,
there are always loads of young
couples in their fifties like us.

*Navigationes non sunt solum pro
senibus, sunt semper multi coniuges
iuvenes consimiles nobis qui habent
inter quinquaginta et sexaginta annos.*

My uncle went to Rome and all I got was
this lousy T-shirt.

*Avunculus meus ivit Roman et ego
cepi solam hanc miseram subuculam.*

No I don't want to buy a
fucking camel ride.

*Non, nolo emere stuprantem
equitationem in camelo.*

Would you like to buy my wife?

Vis emere uxorem meam?

Give me your best price.
That's my final offer.

Dona mihi optimum pretium tuum.
Est ultima condicio mea.

AT THE AIRPORT

Portus Aeris

Any luggage left unattended will be removed and may be destroyed.

Ulla impedimenta relicta abducentur et forte delebuntur.

Do I look like a terrorist to you?

Videor tibi esse factorem terroris?

(At immigration)
This place is amazing.
I'm never going home.

Hoc locus mirus est. Numquam redebo domum.

I have nothing to declare.

Nihil habeo declarare.

It's just for recreational use.

Est solum pro ludo.

If I had something smuggled up my arse,
would you be the person to check?

*Si furtim importarem aliquid
anu meo, exquireresne?*

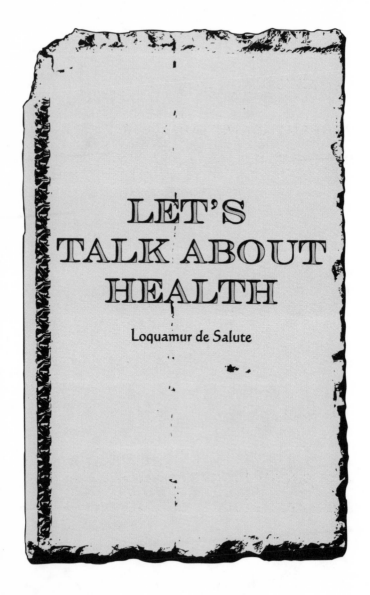

LET'S
TALK ABOUT
HEALTH

Loquamur de Salute

Do crisps count as a major food group?

Habesne solana tuberosa frita et secta magnam partem esse diaetae bonae?

I *am* happy. I had Botox yesterday.

Sum Iucundus. Habui Botox heri.

I'm not a hypochondriac; there are just a lot of things wrong with me.

Non patior morbos fictos; solum habeo malam salutem in multis partibus.

I hate waiting rooms; they make you feel ill.

Odi spatia expectandi;
te aegrum faciunt.

Please don't make me pee into a cup.

Te oro ne me cogas urinam
dare in poculum.

Can you catch bird flu from eating
chicken nuggets?

Potesne capere influenzam avium
edendo portiones pulli in farina frita?

I quit my job so I could go to the gym ten times a week.

Reliqui negotium meum ut irem ad palaestram decies in spatio septem dierum.

You'll just feel a little prick.

Senties solum parvum punctum.

This may be a bit sensitive tomorrow.

Fortasse erit aliquantum molle cras.

I'm addicted to liposuction.

Deditus sum amotione sebi mei suctu.

Tequila and baked beans
just don't mix well.

*Tequila et fabae coctae in forno non
congruunt inter se bene.*

Can you die from man flu?

Potesne mori de influenza hominum?

STUDENT LIFE

LIFE

Vita Studiosorum

My dog ate my USB drive.

Canis meus edit USB meum.

I use lectures to catch up on my sleep.

*Utor scholis somnum
perditum recipere.*

Three years of partying; ten grand of debt.

*Tres anni conviviorum; decem mille
denariorum aeris alieni.*

The tutor is hot.

Praeceptor candens est.

I only date university professors.

Solum habeo assignationes cum professoribus in academia.

This exact same thing happened in *Hollyoaks* last week.

Res ipsa accidit in Quercubus Ilicibus proximo spatio septem dierum.

Do you do student discount?

Facisne deductionem pro stusiosis?

I'm president of the Mind-altering
Substance Society.

*Praefectus sum Societatis Rerum
Quae Mentem Immutant.*

Some people collect stamps – we collect
shopping trolleys and traffic cones.

*Aliqui colligunt signa tabellarii –
nos colligimus plaustra
tabernae et conos viae.*

I have a balanced diet – noodles one day, beans on toast the next.

Diaetam aequam habeo – noodles uno die, fabae in pane tosto proximo die.

I keep empty vodka bottles as a sign of all my university achievements.

Colligo vacuas ampulas aquae muscoviticae signum esse omnium rerum gestarum mearum in academia.

I'm sure they were the best days of my life, although I can't actually remember any of them.

Certus sum eos fuisse dies optimos meae vitae sed non possum recordare ullos eorum.

My pimp stole my homework.

Leno meum furatus est opera domus mea.

Saved by the bell!

Servati tintinnabulo!

I can't go swimming; I appear
to be quite drunk.

*Non possum natare; sum,
videretur, satis ebrius.*

STUDENT RULES

RULES

Regulae Studiosis

Don't do drugs.

Ne feceris pharmaceutica.

Don't have sex. And if you do
have sex, be safe.

*Ne coitum habueris. Et si coitus
habeas, tutus es.*

Were you raised in a barn?

Educatus es in horreo?

Texting the answers to each
other is still cheating.

*Mandare responsa texto
est etiam fraus.*

No masticating in the hallway.

Non licet mandere in atrio.

No alcoholic drinks in the classrooms.

*Nullae potiones quae ebritatem
creant in scholis.*

There's no such word as 'can't'.

Non est verbum 'non possum'.

Rules are *not* made to be broken.

Regulae non *sunt violandae.*

SHOP TILL YOU DROP

Tabernas Perambula Donec Cadas

Do my new boobs go with this dress?

Mammae novae meae congruent cum veste nova mea?

If you want it, buy it...

Si id vis, emi id...

I love a bargain.

Mihi placet bene emere.

A person can never have too many bags.

Homo non potest habere
nimis saccorum.

Shopping is not a hobby; it's a sport.

Non est consuetudo emere; est ludus.

I don't know how people in developing
countries manage without
24-hour supermarkets.

*Non intellego quomodo homines in
terris progredientibus gerere possunt
sine tabernis apertis totum
diem et noctam.*

People with pushchairs shouldn't be
allowed in shops.

*Homines cum sellis impellendis
debent non posse intrare in tabernas.*

If you decide to propose to me, that's the ring I want.

Si statuas proponere nuptias mihi, hic est annulus quem desidero.

Of course I feel bad for the kids who work in sweatshops, but I'd feel worse if no one bought the clothes they made.

Certe misereor puerorum qui laborant in casis sudoris sed peiorem dolorem caperem si nemo emeret vestes quas faciunt.

There's only one cure for the shopaholic.

Una sola medicina est pro homine deditus emendo.

SPORTING TALK

Sermo de Ludis

Goal!

Meta!

Here we go, here we go, here we go...

Nunc imus, nunc imus, nunc imus...

Can we play you every week?

Possumusne ludere vobiscum omne
spatio septem dierum?

You couldn't score in a brothel.

Non potes trahere in ganea.

Who ate all the pies?

Quis edit omnia crusta?

At the end of the day,
it's a game of two halves.

In fine diei, est ludus duarum
aequarum partium.

And England go out of the World Cup
on penalties once again…

*Et Anglica relinquerunt Calicem
Mundi poenis rursus…*

Gladiators were real sportsmen.

Gladadiatores erant veri lusores.

You dirty northern/southern bastard!

*Sordidus nothus de regione
australe/septentrionalis!*

Get up, you pansy, it was only a little kick to the spleen!

Surge cinaede, solum accepisti calcem in splene!

Eng-er-land! Eng-er-land!

An-gli-ca! An-gli-ca!

Go on, my son!

I age, fili mei!

We know where you live, ref.

Cognoscimus ubi vivis, arbiter.

(Sung)
Three lions on a shirt...

Tres leones in tunica...

You're not singing, you're not singing,
you're not singing anymore!

Non canis, non canis,
non canis diutius!

She runs like a girl.

Currit illa modo puellae.

I'd rather forcibly insert a rugby ball up my rectum than lose to those scumbags.

*Malo violenter inserere pilam
Rugbiensem in anum meum
quam vinci illis saccis spumae.*

It certainly looked offside to me.

Certe videretur extra latus mihi.

Gentlemen – start your engines.

Homines generosi –
excitate machinas tuas.

It's only a game.

Solus ludus est.

Get in there, you beauty!

Intra illuc, o pulchra!

Bullseye!

Oculus tauri!

Sofa, check. Pizza, check.
Giant foam finger, check.

Lectus, praesens. Pizza, praesens.
Digitus giganteus factus
spumae, praesens.

THERE'S
NO PLACE
LIKE HOME

Est Nullus Locus Domui Similis

No, I will not spare ten minutes of my valuable time to help your stupid company do market research.

Non, non dabo decem momenta temporis meii adiuvare negotium stultum tuum facere investigationes fori.

You won't miss the beginning of the show, because I can pause live TV.

Non desideras initium spectaculi quod possum sistere televisifica viva.

Do you want Marmite on your toast?

Visne Marmite in pane tuo?

To make this nutritious snack: pierce the
film lid and microwave on full power
for two minutes.

*Facere hanc cenulam in qua multum
alimenti est: perfora operculum
membranae et pone in furno
micro-undis dua momenta.*

I've set up the wireless router so you should be able to get online in the west wing.

Constitui gubernatorem viarum sine filis ut possis ire in telam in ala occidentale.

Everybody report to the living room: the remote control has gone missing again.

Omnes ite ad spatium vivendi: teleimperator est perditus rursus.

The conservatory's lovely in the summer, but then we tend to sit in the garden.

Solarium bellum est in aestate, sed tum solemus sedere in horto.

Will you take the dog out? I have to go on the treadmill.

Canem educesne? Debeo ire in molam currendi.

Will you take the dog to his hairdressing appointment?

Ducisne canem ad constitutum crinis?

I burnt my forehead on my hair straighteners.

Cremavi frontem meam correctoribus crinis.

There's no porn on my computer!

Non est pornographia in computrato meo!

You treat this place like a hotel!

Hunc locum tractas quasi hospitium esset!

Darling, *please* use the safety strap on your Wii control – I don't want to have to replace the TV again this month.

Vita mea, si vis utiris loro salutis imperatoris Wii tui – non volo debere substituere televisificum rursus hoc mense.

GETTING AROUND

Itinera

Don't get me started on public transport...

Non da initium mihi de transvehendo publico...

There's no air conditioning, but you can open the windows.

Non est artificium tractationis aeris, sed potes aperire fenestras.

It's not my fault I'm late, the
satnav took me the long way.

Non est culpa mea quod serus sum,
satnav me duxit longa via.

It's got a built-in sound system, DVD player, LCD TV, mini-fridge and games console, but there's only room for the driver.

Est artificium soni inaedificatum, machina DVD, televisificum LCD, parvum armarium frigidarium et machina communis ludorum sed tantum est spatium pro conductore autocineti.

Open the sunroof, I want to get a tan.

Tectum solis aperi, volo colorare pellem meam.

Why do they call it 'rush hour'
when it lasts two hours?

*Cur vocant id 'horam ruendi'
quando durat duas horas?*

Drive carefully through our village.

Age cura per vicum nostrum.

Buses are like men...

*Autocineta laophora sunt
homiibus consimiles...*

Can I have a return to Tesco please?

Possum habere tesseram redeundi ad Tesco si vis?

Would you like my seat, little old lady?

Visne sella mea, anicula?

All the cool kids sit at the back of the bus.

Omnes pueri urbani sedent in ultima parte autocineti laophori.

The trains are never late!

Hamaxostichi nunquam tardi sunt!

We're sorry for the delay to your journey.

Mora itineris nobis displicet.

Ladies and gentlemen, I'm sorry to inform you that the rail replacement bus service has broken down.

Matronae et homines generosi, mihi displicet tibi dicere autocinetum laophorum in loco hamaxostichi deficisse.

(Shouted into a mobile phone)
I'm on the train!

Sum in hamaxosticho!

May I have some overpriced
refreshments from the trolley?

Possumne habere refectiones
immodico pretio de plaustro?

I like to drive my car into cyclists who don't
wear helmets – it teaches them a lesson.

Mihi placet autocinetum agere in
birotarios qui non portant
galeas – docet eos.

I'm 50. I bought a motorbike. I wear a leather jacket. I am *not* having a mid-life crisis.

Quinquaginta annos habeo. Emi birotarium autocinetum. Porto tunicam scorteam. Non habeo discrimen mediae vitae.

I *have* fastened my seat belt and returned my seat to its full upright and uncomfortable position.

Connexui zonam sellae meam et reduxi sellam meam ad locum totum rectum et incommodum.

We seem to be experiencing
some turbulence.

Videmur experiri tumultus aliquos.

Have you ever skydived? Well, when
we crash it'll be like that, but
without the parachute.

Umquam urinatus es de caelo?
Quando ad terram cademus,
erit consimile illo sed sine
umbella descensoria.

Are you a member of the mile-high club?

Sodalis es societatis mille altae?

The problem with the private jet is that
you don't get a complimentary
eye mask or headphones.

*Quaestio cum aeroplanis propriis est
quod non adducis personam
oculorum libram aut
cephalophonia.*

LIFESTYLE
AND THE
ENVIRONMENT

Modus Vitae et Statio Mundi

The 4x4 was bad for the environment, so
now we drop the kids off at school
in the helicopter.

*Autocinetum cum quattor rotis
agentibus erat noxium, nunc ergo
afferimus pueros ad scholam in
aeroplano cum ala singula
agente in orbem.*

If they make petrol cheaper, then more
people will be able to afford organic
vegetables: being green is about
give and take.

*Si faciunt petrolium viliorem, plures
gentes poterunt emere holera organica:
viriditas est dare et capere.*

We recycle everything.

Utimur omnibus rebus rursus.

We only grow organic.

Solum colimus organica.

The solar panels are for
running the windmill.

Tabulae solis sunt utendo mola venti.

Don't leave your carbon footprints all over
my new fair trade carpets.

*Ne reliqueris vestigia tua carbonis
passim in novis tapetis meis
commercii aequi.*

WATER-COOLER CONVERSATION

Sermones Prope Machinam Aquae Gelidae

Latin guy: That new celebrity reality TV
show starts this week.
Latin chick: Who's in it?
Latin guy: No one famous.

*Homo Latinus: Illud novum
spectaculum rerum verarum cum
hominibus famosis incipit proximo
spatio septem dierum.
Puella Latina: Quis inest?
Homo Latinus: Nemo famosus.*

Of course I can come to your wedding; I'll
just Sky+ the *Eastenders* omnibus.

*Certe possum venire ad nuptias tuas;
solum utar Sky+ memoriae mandare
omnibus* Eastenders.

There's this five-year-old boy in Russia somewhere, who's so fat his friends roll him to school.

Est puer in terra Muscovita aliquo qui habet quinque annos et qui tam obesus est ut amici sui volvant eum ad scholam.

Did you hear about that dog that walks on two legs?

Audivistisne de cane qui ambulat duobus cruribus?

Did you know that British firms waste £43 billion a year on water-cooler conversations?

Cognovistisne negotia Britannica perdere quadraginta et tres milies decies centena in sermonibus ad machinam frigidariam aquae?

Did you see the game last night?

Vidistisne ludum heri nocte?

You'll never guess who's had their boobs done!

Numquam divinas qui habet mammas novas!

I know she looks pregnant, but
she's just really fat.

*Cognosco eam pregnantem videri
sed re ipsa tantum obesa est.*

Make sure you ask lots of questions in the
health and safety seminar so we don't
have to go back to work.

*Pone multas quaesitiones in conventu
de salute ut non debeamus
redire ad opera.*

Does anyone have a condom?

Habetne aliquis condom?

Did you get my e-mail about
Andrew's hair?

*Recepistine mandatum telae meum
de crine Andreae?*

Excuse me, could I get some
water please?

*Excusa me, possum capere
aquam si vis?*

Any ideas for the office party theme?
I was thinking Hawaiian.

*Ullae cogitationes pro proposito
convivi tabularii? Putabam Hawaiian.*

... And his penis is really small... What? He's standing right behind me, isn't he?

... Et penis eius est vere parvus... Quid? Est a tergo meo, non est?

I love your shoes!

Amo calceos tuos!

How can it be out of order *again*?

Quomodo potest non operari rursus*?*

WORK IN PROGRESS

Opus Progrediens

The spam today is ridiculous.
Spam, spam, spam.

*Spam hodie est ridiculosus.
Spam, spam, spam.*

Cartridge error – please consult
your user manual.

*Error ampullae atramenti – sis adi
librum institutionis tuum.*

Please insert paper into printer tray.

*Sis insere chartas in
ferculum imprimoris.*

Do you think this milk is off?
It looks green.

Putasne hunc lactem putridum esse?
Videtur viridem esse.

Anyone fancy getting pissed over lunch?

Quisquam vult bibere ad
ebrietatem in prandio?

Did you see the boss dancing at the
Christmas party?

Visistine dominum saltare in
convivio pro Saturnalibus?

This is a memo to remind everyone to check the memo sent out this morning that disclosed the new memo protocol.

Hoc est memorandum admonere omnes observare memorandum emissum mane hodie quod patefecit novam regulam memorandorum.

Are you chatting on MSN instead of working too?

Tu quoque garris in MSN in loco laborandi?

I'm not sure about that one, Bob, you'll have to check with human resources.

Non certus sum de illa re, Bob, debebis interrogare munus auxiliorum humanorum.

We've set up a focus group to analyse the results from last week's focus group.

Constituimus circulum dedicatum explicando fructus de circulo dedicato spatii septem dierum proximi.

Great PowerPoint presentation, Jan, sorry for falling asleep.

Mirum spectaculum PowerPoint, Jan, me paenitet me cecidisse in somnum.

Ready for the teleconference at nine?

Parati estis pro teleconventu novem hora?

I'm already up to speed, I read the e-mail on my Blackberry.

Cognitum est mihi, legi mandatum telae in Rubo Fructicoso meo.

Let's do lunch!

Faciamus prandium!

I can't make it: I've got a client meeting.

Non possum venire: habeo conventum cum emptoribus.

A company pays us to pay someone else to find someone to carry out research for them – it's very rewarding work.

Negotium dona pecuniam nobis invenire aliquem facere investigationes eis – est negotium valde remunerans.

I'm calling in sick tomorrow, there's a double bill of *Deal or No Deal?*

Cras dicam me esse aegrum, est spectaculum duplex de Negotium aut non Negotium?

I slept with Becky from accounts and never called her back. I still haven't got my pay cheque.

Concubui Becky de munere rationum et numquam dedi salutationem telephonii ei. Adhuc non recepi perscriptionem stipendii meam.

Have you seen the new work experience girl? She's hot!

Visistine novam puellam experientiae laboris? Candens est!

Could someone help me? I seem to have got my tie caught in the paper shredder.

Aliquisne potest adiuvare me? Videor implicavisse nodum meum in secatore chartae.

Don't crash... please don't crash...
I'll do anything...

*Ne cecidistis de caelo... ne cecideris
de caelo... Faciam aliquid...*

WORLD VIEWS

VIEWS

Sententiae de Mundo

Size zero models are humanitarians.

Exemplares vestium qui portant magnitudinem nihil philanthropi sunt.

Yes, it must suck living in poverty, but we all have our problems.

Vero, certe est miserabile vivere in angustis rebus, sed nos omnes habent difficultates.

He spoke to me on the Tube so I figured he had to be a terrorist.

Locutus est mecum in hamaxosticho in Tubo, ergo divinavi eum factorem terroris esse.

Traffic wardens are the spawn of Satan.

Custodes viarum sunt nati Satana.

British hospitals are more generous than any other in the world. Where else can you go in with one bug and come out with two?

Valetudinaria Britannica sunt meliora quam ulli alii in mundo. Quo alio loco potes intrare cum uno morbo et discedere cum alio?

Make love, not war.

Facite amorem, non bellum.

The whole big bang theory is such a joke
– don't you think we would have heard it?

*Doctrina magnae explosionis est
tantus iocus – nonne putas nos
audivisse id!*

If we have been visited by extraterrestrial
life, why didn't they kill us all when
they had the chance?

*Si visitati sumus ab hominibus
de alia stella errante, cur non
occiderunt nos statim!*

Global warming – bring it on! An all-year tan and a shorter drive to the beach!

Calefactio mundi – veniat! Colorandum pellem totum annum et via brevior ad litus!

I don't *do* politics.

Non tracto res publicas.

I just don't get it; why buy a muddy misshapen carrot when you can get one that shines?

Non intellego; cur emas daucum carotam luteum et deformem quando potes emere carotam quae nitet?

Let's go round there and take their TVs.
Why should debt collecting from the
Third World be any different?

*Adeamus illuc et capiamus televisifica
eorum. Cur debet diversum esse
colligere aes alienum de terris
de Tertio Mundo?*

In my day we used to collect empty drinks
bottles. Youth today collect ASBOs.

*In iuventute mea, solebamus colligere
ampullas vacuas. Iuvenes hodie
colligunt mandata ASBO.*

I'm sure that if all the world leaders came together for a nice chat over a good brew, a lot of this shit would get sorted.

Si omnes duces mundi conveniant ad bonum sermonem bonis potionibus multum de hoc excremento remediatur.

The rain in Spain falls mainly on England.

Imber in Hispania cadit plerumque in Anglica.

Going green is just an excuse for not washing.

Fieri viridis non est excusantium pro non lavando.

Pigeons are rats with wings.

Columbae sunt mures alis.

This is a bus stop, not a brothel.

*Intermissio autocineti laophori
est, non ganea.*

Prison's just like a five-star hotel these days.

*Carcer est similis hospitio
quinque stellis hodie.*

Bring back public hangings!

Reduce suspendia publica!

Why can't we just all be friends?

Cur non omnes possumus amici esse?

Mummy, I'm going to leave my vegetables. I'll send them to the starving kids in Africa if it bothers you so much.

Mater, relinquam holera mea. Mittam ea ad pueros consumptos fame in Africa si te paenitet tantum.

Maybe reality TV is the true actuality of existence and the rest of us are living a lie.

Fortasse televisificum veritatis est verus modus existentiae et alli nostri vivimus in mendacio.

If you're feeling bad about life,
eat chocolate.

Si putas vitam malam esse,
edi chocolatam.

I miss the colonial times when you could
rock up onto an island and claim
it as your own.

Desidero dies coloniarum quando
potebatis se in terram exponere in
insula et capere eam sibi.

I live life on the edge.

Vivo in acie.

OTHER USELESS PHRASES

Aliae Locutiones Inutiles

Am I bovvered?

Sollicitusne sum?

You've got to be in it to win it.

Debes inesse vincere.

Well, this is it you see...

Bene, hoc est vide...

No thanks, we already
have double glazing.

*Non gratias, iam habemus
vitrum duplicem.*

It's quality, not quantity.

Natura est, non quantitas.

What do you think you're looking at?

Quod putas te observare?

Speak to the hand.

Loqui manu.

In my day...

In die meo...

Does my bum look big in this?

*Clunesne meae viderentur
magnae in hac?*

I love you.

Te amo.

You don't get a word I'm saying, do you, you non-Latin speaking cretin!

Non intelleges solum verbum quod dico, intellegesne, asine qui non lingua Latina utiris!

The tail seems to be wagging the dog here.

Cauda videretur movere canem hic.

Supersize me.

Magna magnitudo mihi.

No, I don't want insurance for my mobile.

Non, non volo fidem de damno resarciendo interpositam telephonii mobilis meii.

Don't call us, we'll call you.

Non vocate nos, vocabimus vos.

The more the merrier.

Plures sunt iucundiores.

The name's Bond. James Bond.

Nomen est Bond. James Bond.

Your call is important to us.

Salutatio vestra multum valet nobis.

Your call is being held in a queue.

Salutatio vestra tenetur in linea.

Why did the chicken cross the road?

Cur pullus transivit viam?

Where are the toilets?

Ubi sunt latrinae?

At the end of the day...

In fine diei...

Oh, you want to borrow this book?
Buy your own copy!

Visne mutuari librum?
Emi exemplum vestrum!

Who says Latin is a dead language?

Quis dicit linguam Latinam
mortuam esse?

www.summersdale.com